MW00976853

# Four Weeks:
# The Steadfast Love of God

*edited by Wendy Alsup*
*All Scripture from The Holy Bible, English Standard Version® (ESV®)*
*Copyright © 2001 by Crossway,*
*a publishing ministry of Good News Publishers.*
*All rights reserved.*
*ESV Text Edition: 2007*

# Week 1

*God declares His steadfast love in what may seem to us a surprising context—the giving of His Law to His children to set up their culture, their way of relating to each other, and their way of relating to God.*

*Day 1*


Exodus 15:13
You have led in your steadfast love the people whom
you have redeemed; you have guided them by your
strength to your holy abode.


Exodus 20:6
but showing steadfast love to thousands of those who
love me and keep my commandments.

*Reflections*:

_____

_____

_____

_____

_____

_____

_____

_____

_____

_____

_____

_____

_____

_____

_____

_____

_____

_____

_____

_____

_____

_____

_____

*Day 2*

Exodus 34:6
The Lord passed before him and proclaimed, "The
Lord, the Lord, a God merciful and gracious, slow to
anger, and abounding in steadfast love and
faithfulness,"


Numbers 14:19
Please pardon the iniquity of this people, according to
the greatness of your steadfast love, just as you have
forgiven this people, from Egypt until now.

*Reflections*:

*Day 3*

Deuteronomy 5:10
but showing steadfast love to thousands of those who
love me and keep my commandments.


Deuteronomy 7:8
but it is because the Lord loves you and is keeping the
oath that he swore to your fathers, that the Lord has
brought you out with a mighty hand and redeemed
you from the house of slavery, from the hand of
Pharaoh king of Egypt.

*Reflections*:

_____

_____

_____

_____

_____

_____

_____

_____

_____

_____

_____

_____

_____

_____

_____

_____

_____

_____

_____

_____

_____

_____

*Day 4*

Deuteronomy 7:13
He will love you, bless you, and multiply you. He
will also bless the fruit of your womb and the fruit of
your ground, your grain and your wine and your oil,
the increase of your herds and the young of your
flock, in the land that he swore to your fathers to give
you.


Deuteronomy 10:15
Yet the Lord set his heart in love on your fathers and
chose their offspring after them, you above all
peoples, as you are this day.

*Reflections*:

_____

_____

_____

_____

_____

_____

_____

_____

_____

_____

_____

_____

_____

_____

_____

_____

_____

_____

_____

_____

_____

_____

_____

_____

*Day 5*

Deuteronomy 10:18
He executes justice for the fatherless and the widow, and loves the sojourner, giving him food and clothing.

Deuteronomy 23:5
But the Lord your God would not listen to Balaam; instead the Lord your God turned the curse into a blessing for you, because the Lord your God loved you.

*Reflections*:

_____

_____

_____

_____

_____

_____

_____

_____

_____

_____

_____

_____

_____

_____

_____

_____

_____

_____

_____

_____

_____

_____

_____

# Week 2

*God's steadfast love is a repeated theme in the songbook of Israel.*

*Day 1*

Psalm 13:5
But I have trusted in your steadfast love; my heart
shall rejoice in your salvation.

Psalm 25:10
All the paths of the Lord are steadfast love and
faithfulness, for those who keep his covenant and his
testimonies.

Psalm 31:7
I will rejoice and be glad in your steadfast love,
because you have seen my affliction; you have known
the distress of my soul,

Psalm 31:21
Blessed be the Lord, for he has wondrously shown his
steadfast love to me when I was in a besieged city.

Psalm 33:18
Behold, the eye of the Lord is on those who fear him,
on those who hope in his steadfast love,

*Reflections*:

_____

_____

_____

_____

_____

_____

_____

_____

_____

_____

_____

_____

_____

_____

_____

_____

_____

_____

_____

_____

_____

_____

_____

*Day 2*

Psalm 33:22
Let your steadfast love, O Lord, be upon us, even as
we hope in you.

Psalm 36:7
How precious is your steadfast love, O God! The
children of mankind take refuge in the shadow of
your wings.

Psalm 40:11
As for you, O Lord, you will not restrain your mercy
from me; your steadfast love and your faithfulness
will ever preserve me!

Psalm 52:8
But I am like a green olive tree in the house of God. I
trust in the steadfast love of God forever and ever.

Psalm 59:16 - 17
But I will sing of your strength; I will sing aloud of
your steadfast love in the morning. For you have been
to me a fortress and a refuge in the day of my distress.
O my Strength, I will sing praises to you, for you, O
God, are my fortress, the God who shows me
steadfast love.

*Reflections*:

_____

_____

_____

_____

_____

_____

_____

_____

_____

_____

_____

_____

_____

_____

_____

_____

_____

_____

_____

_____

_____

_____

*Day 3*

Psalm 63:3
Because your steadfast love is better than life, my lips will praise you.

Psalm 66:20
Blessed be God, because he has not rejected my prayer or removed his steadfast love from me!

Psalm 86:5
For you, O Lord, are good and forgiving, abounding in steadfast love to all who call upon you.

Psalm 89:14
Righteousness and justice are the foundation of your throne; steadfast love and faithfulness go before you.

Psalm 94:18
When I thought, "My foot slips," your steadfast love, O Lord, held me up.

*Reflections*:

_____
_____
_____
_____
_____
_____
_____
_____
_____
_____
_____
_____
_____
_____
_____
_____
_____
_____
_____
_____
_____
_____

*Day 4*

Psalm 100:5
For the Lord is good; his steadfast love endures
forever, and his faithfulness to all generations.

Psalm 103:4
who redeems your life from the pit, who crowns you
with steadfast love and mercy,

Psalm 103:8
The Lord is merciful and gracious, slow to anger and
abounding in steadfast love.

Psalm 103:11
For as high as the heavens are above the earth, so
great is his steadfast love toward those who fear him;

Psalm 107:43
Whoever is wise, let him attend to these things; let
them consider the steadfast love of the Lord.

Psalm 117:2
For great is his steadfast love toward us, and the
faithfulness of the Lord endures forever. Praise the
Lord!

*Reflections*:

*Day 5*

Psalm 119:64
The earth, O Lord, is full of your steadfast love; teach me your statutes!

Psalm 119:76
Let your steadfast love comfort me according to your promise to your servant.

Psalm 143:8
Let me hear in the morning of your steadfast love, for in you I trust. Make me know the way I should go, for to you I lift up my soul.

Psalm 145:8
The Lord is gracious and merciful, slow to anger and abounding in steadfast love.

Psalm 147:11
but the Lord takes pleasure in those who fear him, in those who hope in his steadfast love.

*Reflections*:

_____

_____

_____

_____

_____

_____

_____

_____

_____

_____

_____

_____

_____

_____

_____

_____

_____

_____

_____

_____

_____

_____

# Week 3

*God's hand of discipline does not negate His love for us, and, in fact, proves it. God's children are sustained through captivity and return to obedience by remembering God's steadfast love.*

*Day 1*

Ezra 3:11
And they sang responsively, praising and giving thanks to the Lord, "For he is good, for his steadfast love endures forever toward Israel." And all the people shouted with a great shout when they praised the Lord, because the foundation of the house of the Lord was laid.

Ezra 7:28
and who extended to me his steadfast love before the king and his counselors, and before all the king's mighty officers. I took courage, for the hand of the Lord my God was on me, and I gathered leading men from Israel to go up with me.

Ezra 9:9
For we are slaves. Yet our God has not forsaken us in our slavery, but has extended to us his steadfast love before the kings of Persia, to grant us some reviving to set up the house of our God, to repair its ruins, and to give us protection in Judea and Jerusalem.

*Reflections*:

_____

_____

_____

_____

_____

_____

_____

_____

_____

_____

_____

_____

_____

_____

_____

_____

_____

_____

_____

_____

_____

*Day 2*

Nehemiah 1:5
And I said, "O Lord God of heaven, the great and awesome God who keeps covenant and steadfast love with those who love him and keep his commandments,"

Nehemiah 9:17
They refused to obey and were not mindful of the wonders that you performed among them, but they stiffened their neck and appointed a leader to return to their slavery in Egypt. But you are a God ready to forgive, gracious and merciful, slow to anger and abounding in steadfast love, and did not forsake them.

*Reflections:*

_____

_____

_____

_____

_____

_____

_____

_____

_____

_____

_____

_____

_____

_____

_____

_____

_____

_____

_____

_____

_____

*Day 3*

Proverbs 3:12
for the Lord reproves him whom he loves, as a father the son in whom he delights.

Isaiah 54:10
For the mountains may depart and the hills be removed, but my steadfast love shall not depart from you, and my covenant of peace shall not be removed," says the Lord, who has compassion on you.

Isaiah 63:7
I will recount the steadfast love of the Lord, the praises of the Lord, according to all that the Lord has granted us, and the great goodness to the house of Israel that he has granted them according to his compassion, according to the abundance of his steadfast love.

*Reflections*:

_____

_____

_____

_____

_____

_____

_____

_____

_____

_____

_____

_____

_____

_____

_____

_____

_____

_____

_____

_____

_____

_____

*Day 4*

Lamentations 3:22
The steadfast love of the Lord never ceases; his mercies never come to an end;

Lamentations 3:32
but, though he cause grief, he will have compassion according to the abundance of his steadfast love;

Hosea 2:19
And I will betroth you to me forever. I will betroth you to me in righteousness and in justice, in steadfast love and in mercy.

*Reflections:*

_____

_____

_____

_____

_____

_____

_____

_____

_____

_____

_____

_____

_____

_____

_____

_____

_____

_____

_____

_____

_____

*Day 5*

Micah 7:18
Who is a God like you, pardoning iniquity and
passing over transgression for the remnant of his
inheritance? He does not retain his anger forever,
because he delights in steadfast love.


Zephaniah 3:17
The Lord your God is in your midst, a mighty one
who will save; he will rejoice over you with gladness;
he will quiet you by his love; he will exult over you
with loud singing.

*Reflections*:

_____

_____

_____

_____

_____

_____

_____

_____

_____

_____

_____

_____

_____

_____

_____

_____

_____

_____

_____

_____

_____

_____

# Week 4

*In the New Testament, Jesus reaffirms God's love for us in Him. The Apostle Paul gives the great treatise on God's unfailing love from which nothing can separate us.*

*Day 1*

John 3:16
"For God so loved the world, that he gave his only
Son, that whoever believes in him should not perish
but have eternal life."


John 15:12
"This is my commandment, that you love one another
as I have loved you."


John 15:13
Greater love has no one than this, that someone lay
down his life for his friends.

*Reflections*:

_____
_____
_____
_____
_____
_____
_____
_____
_____
_____
_____
_____
_____
_____
_____
_____
_____
_____
_____
_____
_____
_____
_____

*Day 2*

Romans 1:7
To all those in Rome who are loved by God and
called to be saints: Grace to you and peace from God
our Father and the Lord Jesus Christ.


Romans 5:5
and hope does not put us to shame, because God's
love has been poured into our hearts through the Holy
Spirit who has been given to us.


Romans 5:8
but God shows his love for us in that while we were
still sinners, Christ died for us.

*Reflections*:

*Day 3*

Romans 8:35 - 39
Who shall separate us from the love of Christ? Shall tribulation, or distress, or persecution, or famine, or nakedness, or danger, or sword? ...

No, in all these things we are more than conquerors through him who loved us. For I am sure that neither death nor life, nor angels nor rulers, nor things present nor things to come, nor powers, nor height nor depth, nor anything else in all creation, will be able to separate us from the love of God in Christ Jesus our Lord.

*Reflections:*

_____

_____

_____

_____

_____

_____

_____

_____

_____

_____

_____

_____

_____

_____

_____

_____

_____

_____

_____

_____

_____

_____

_____

*Day 4*

Ephesians 5:2
And walk in love, as Christ loved us and gave himself
up for us, a fragrant offering and sacrifice to God.


2 Thessalonians 2:16-17
Now may our Lord Jesus Christ himself, and God our
Father, who loved us and gave us eternal comfort and
good hope through grace, comfort your hearts and
establish them in every good work and word.

*Reflections*:

_____

_____

_____

_____

_____

_____

_____

_____

_____

_____

_____

_____

_____

_____

_____

_____

_____

_____

_____

_____

_____

_____

_____

*Day 5*

*Review this booklet and refresh yourself with verses that particularly stood out to you. Here are some questions to consider for your reflections.*

*What has God spoken to you through His Word about His posture toward you?*

*How would you define God's steadfast love?*

*How does does God's love impact how you view yourself?*

*What words would you use to describe your relationship with God in light of this love?*

*How does this love equip you to live boldly and obediently in your particular circumstances?*

*How does God's unfailing love for you equip you to face and work through your own sins or failures?*

*Reflections:*

_____

_____

_____

_____

_____

_____

_____

_____

_____

_____

_____

_____

_____

_____

_____

_____

_____

_____

_____

_____

_____

_____

Made in the USA
Columbia, SC
13 February 2025

53782275R00031